NORTH AMERICAN ANIMALS

# Bald Eagles

by Chris Bowman

BLASTOFF! READERS
3

BELLWETHER MEDIA • MINNEAPOLIS, MN

Note to Librarians, Teachers, and Parents:

**Blastoff! Readers** are carefully developed by literacy experts and combine standards-based content with developmentally appropriate text.

**Level 1** provides the most support through repetition of high-frequency words, light text, predictable sentence patterns, and strong visual support.

**Level 2** offers early readers a bit more challenge through varied simple sentences, increased text load, and less repetition of high-frequency words.

**Level 3** advances early-fluent readers toward fluency through increased text and concept load, less reliance on visuals, longer sentences, and more literary language.

**Level 4** builds reading stamina by providing more text per page, increased use of punctuation, greater variation in sentence patterns, and increasingly challenging vocabulary.

**Level 5** encourages children to move from "learning to read" to "reading to learn" by providing even more text, varied writing styles, and less familiar topics.

Whichever book is right for your reader, Blastoff! Readers are the perfect books to build confidence and encourage a love of reading that will last a lifetime!

This edition first published in 2015 by Bellwether Media, Inc.

No part of this publication may be reproduced in whole or in part without written permission of the publisher. For information regarding permission, write to Bellwether Media, Inc., Attention: Permissions Department, 5357 Penn Avenue South, Minneapolis, MN 55419.

Library of Congress Cataloging-in-Publication Data

Bowman, Chris, 1990- author.
  Bald Eagles / by Chris Bowman.
     pages cm. – (Blastoff! Readers. North American Animals)
  Includes bibliographical references and index.
  Summary: "Simple text and full-color photography introduce beginning readers to bald eagles. Developed by literacy experts for students in kindergarten through third grade"– Provided by publisher.
  Audience: Ages 5-8.
  Audience: K to Grade 3.
  ISBN 978-1-62617-185-5 (hardcover : alk. paper)
  1. Bald eagle–Juvenile literature.  I. Title.
  QL696.F32B667 2015
  598.9'43–dc23
                          2014042095

Printed in the United States of America, North Mankato, MN.

# Table of **Contents**

# What Are Bald Eagles?

Bald eagles are one of the largest **raptors** in North America. The birds are an American **symbol**.

N
W E
S

Extinct

Extinct in the Wild

Critically Endangered

Endangered

Vulnerable

Near Threatened

Least Concern

bald eagle range = 

conservation status: least concern

They fly over much of Canada, the United States, and parts of northern Mexico.

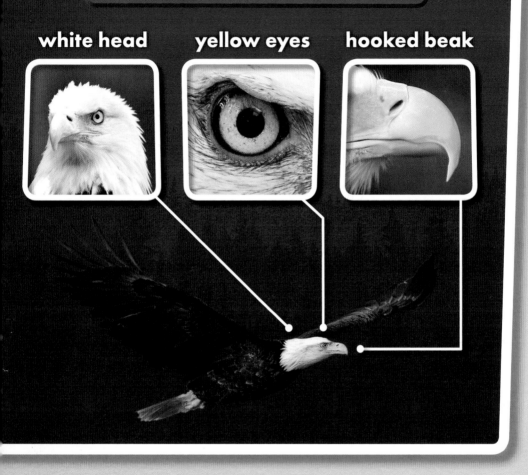

## Identify a Bald Eagle

white head   yellow eyes   hooked beak

Bald eagles have brown feathers on their bodies and wings. The white feathers on their heads make them look bald.

Their beaks, legs, and feet
are yellow.

Females grow larger than males. They are up to 3 feet (0.9 meters) tall. Most weigh about 14 pounds (6.4 kilograms).

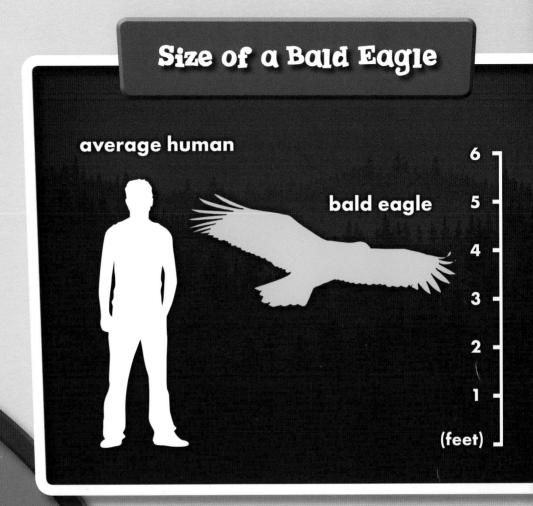

## Size of a Bald Eagle

average human

bald eagle

6
5
4
3
2
1
(feet)

The eagles' wings spread out to be about 7 feet (2.1 meters).

# Nesting and Hunting

Bald eagles build their nests near rivers, lakes, and marshes. Some nest near the coast.

Nests are made of sticks, grasses, and moss. They are often 6 feet (1.8 meters) wide and 4 feet (1.2 meters) high. Most nests are at the tops of tall trees.

Bald eagles **perch** on high branches to hunt for rabbits and snakes. These **carnivores** soar above water to find fish and ducks.

salmon

catfish

muskrats

mallard ducks

cottontail
rabbits

western diamondback
rattlesnakes

They eat **carrion** and steal food
from other birds, too.

13

In winter, bald eagles gather in large groups. They wait by open water for **prey**.

Some **migrate** to warmer areas to find food.

Male and female bald eagles have special **courtship displays**. A pair will lock **talons** high in the sky.

Then they spin while falling. They let go at the last second to avoid crashing.

A female lays up to three eggs at a time. Mom and dad take turns keeping the eggs warm. **Eaglets** hatch after about a month.

## Baby Facts

| | |
|---|---|
| Name for babies: | eaglets |
| Number of eggs laid: | 1 to 3 eggs |
| Time spent inside egg: | 35 days |
| Time spent with parents: | 4 to 5 months |

Eaglets hop in their nest and flap their wings. Soon they jump between branches.

At about 12 weeks old, they take their first flight. They have become **fledglings**!

# Glossary

**carnivores**—animals that only eat meat

**carrion**—the rotting meat of a dead animal

**courtship displays**—behaviors that animals perform when choosing mates

**eaglets**—baby eagles

**fledglings**—young birds that have feathers for flight

**migrate**—to travel from one place to another, often with the seasons

**perch**—to sit in a high place

**prey**—animals that are hunted by other animals for food

**raptors**—large birds that hunt other animals; raptors have excellent eyesight and powerful talons.

**symbol**—an animal or object that represents something else

**talons**—the strong, sharp claws of bald eagles and other raptors

# To Learn More

### AT THE LIBRARY
George, Jean Craighead. *The Eagles Are Back.* New York, N.Y.: Dial Books for Young Readers, 2013.

Magby, Meryl. *Bald Eagles.* New York, N.Y.: PowerKids Press, 2012.

Monroe, Tyler. *The Bald Eagle.* North Mankato, Minn.: Capstone Press, 2014.

### ON THE WEB
Learning more about bald eagles is as easy as 1, 2, 3.

1. Go to www.factsurfer.com.

2. Enter "bald eagles" into the search box.

3. Click the "Surf" button and you will see a list of related web sites.

With factsurfer.com, finding more information is just a click away.

# Index

The images in this book are reproduced through the courtesy of: schweingrubers, front cover; Alaska Stock/ SuperStock, pp. 4-5; Mircea Bezergheanu, p. 6 (top left); KarSol, p. 6 (top center); Mayskyphoto, p. 6 (top right); FloridaStock, p. 6 (bottom); Chris Humphries, p. 7; Rosalie Kreulen, pp. 8-9; Mark Newman/ Getty Images, pp. 10, 11, 20; Bucks Wildlife Photography/ Getty Images, pp. 12-13 (top); Menno Schaefer, pp. 12-13 (bottom); StudioSmart, p. 13 (top left); Volosina, p. 13 (top right); Sergey Uryadnikov, p. 13 (center left); Christian Musat, p. 13 (center right); Michael Chatt, p. 13 (bottom left); Audrey Snider-Bell, p. 13 (bottom right); Frank Lukasseck/ Corbis, pp. 14-15; Aurora Open/ SuperStock, pp. 16-17 (top); Pakhnyushch, pp. 16-17 (bottom); Bird Images, pp. 18-19; predrag1, p. 19; Anatoliy Lukich, p. 21.